David Cumming

Please visit our web site at: www.worldalmanaclibrary.com
For a free color catalog describing World Almanac® Library's list of high-quality books and multimedia programs, call 1-800-848-2928 (USA) or 1-800-387-3178 (Canada). World Almanac® Library's fax: (414) 332-3567.

Library of Congress Cataloging-in-Publication Data

Cumming, David.
The Nile / David Cumming.
p. cm. — (Great rivers of the world)
Includes bibliographical references and index.
Contents: The course of the river — The Nile in history — Cities and settlements — Farming, trade, and industry — Animals and plants — Environmental issues — Leisure and recreation — The future.
ISBN 0-8368-5445-4 (lib. bdg.)
ISBN 0-8368-5452-7 (softcover)
1. Nile River Valley—Juvenile literature. 2. Nile River—Juvenile literature. [1. Nile River. 2. Nile River Valley.] I. Title. II. Series.
DT116.C86 2003
962—dc21 2002033139

First published in 2003 by
World Almanac® Library
330 West Olive Street, Suite 100
Milwaukee, WI 53212 USA

Developed by Monkey Puzzle Media
Editor: Jane Bingham
Designer: Tim Mayer
Picture researcher: Lynda Lines
World Almanac® Library editor: Jim Mezzanotte
World Almanac® Library art direction: Tammy Gruenewald

Picture acknowledgements
AKG London, 12 (Erich Lessing), 14; Corbis, 21 (Paul Amasy), 30–31 (Peter Johnson), 34 (William Dow), 36–37 (Adam Woolfitt); Corbis Digital Stock, 40; Digital Vision, 33; FLPA, 7; Impact, 28 (Colin Jones); Mark Henley, 4, 19, 24, 44; Mary Evans Picture Library, 15, 17; NASA, 9; Robert Harding Picture Library, 5 (David Beatty), 8 (Julia Bayne), 13 (Ellen Rooney), 20, 22 (Trevor Wood), 25 (Guy Thouvenin), 26 (Julia Bayne), 42 (D. Jacobs), 43 (E. Simanor); Still Pictures, cover (Jorgen Schytte), 11 (Michael Schwerberger/DAS Fotoarchiv), 23 (Hartmut Schwarzbach), 27 (Shehzad Noorani), 29 (Andreas Riedmiller/DAS Fotoarchiv), 32 (M. & C. Denis-Huot/Bios), 35 (M. & C. Denis-Huot); Travel Ink, 1 (Peter Kingsford), 39 (Peter Kingsford). Map artwork by Peter Bull.

Printed in the United States of America

1 2 3 4 5 6 7 8 9 07 06 05 04 03

CONTENTS

INTRODUCTION

The Longest River

The Nile River in Africa is the world's longest river. It is formed by two branches, the White Nile and the Blue Nile. The **source** of the White Nile, in the central African country of Burundi, is farther from the sea. From this source, the White Nile flows north through Tanzania, Rwanda, Uganda, and Sudan. At the city of Khartoum, the White Nile is joined by the Blue Nile, which flows into Sudan from the mountains of Ethiopia. The Nile River begins at the confluence, or coming together, of these two branches. From Sudan, the river flows north through Egypt to the Mediterranean Sea.

The Nile's total length is measured from the source of the White Nile to the **mouth** of the river in the Mediterranean Sea. It is 4,132 miles (6,650 kilometers) long — 127 miles (204 km) longer than the Amazon River in South America, the world's second longest river.

Nile Facts

- Length: 4,132 miles (6,650 km)
- Drainage basin: 1,293,000 sq miles (3,349,000 sq km)
- Main cities: Alexandria (Egypt), Aswan (Egypt), Cairo (Egypt), Khartoum (Sudan), Khartoum North (Sudan), Luxor (Egypt), Omdurman (Sudan)
- Delta width: 155 miles (250 km)
- Major tributaries: Atbarah, 800 miles (1,287 km), Sobat, 460 miles (740 km)

Egyptian farmers use the land on either side of the Nile River for farming. The desert begins at the pyramids in the background.

The Nile has many smaller rivers, known as **tributaries**, flowing into it. Together, the Nile and its tributaries drain water from a huge area known as the Nile **basin**. The Nile River's basin covers one-tenth of the African continent.

The Nile River and Egypt

The Nile River and its two branches pass through seven countries. Of these countries, Egypt is most in need of the river's water. Much of Egypt is desert and gets very little rain. People have been living in Egypt for thousands of years, however, because the Nile River brings water. The Nile has also provided Egyptians with rich farmland. Until the twentieth century, the river flooded the land on either side of it once a year, leaving behind a layer of muddy **silt**. Fed by water from the Nile, crops have grown well in this fertile soil.

Sharing the Nile?

The Egyptians of today depend on the Nile for their survival, just as the ancient Egyptians did thousands of years ago. Today, however, Sudan and Ethiopia also need the Nile's water. With the populations of these three countries growing fast, millions more will soon need water, but the amount of water in the river is limited. In the twenty-first century, conflicts may develop as these countries all compete for the Nile River's precious resource.

After leaving Lake Tana in Ethiopia, the waters of the Blue Nile flow northward.

Chapter 1

THE COURSE OF THE RIVER

THE COURSE OF THE RIVER

This map shows the course of the Nile and its main tributaries.

The First Nile

Thirty million years ago, the river we now call the Nile was much shorter than it is today. Like the modern Nile, this early river emptied into the Mediterranean Sea, but it began north of present-day Khartoum. The river was separated from Lake Victoria, which lay to the south, by an enormous, prehistoric body of water called Lake Sudd.

About 25,000 years ago, a river began to flow out of Lake Victoria and into Lake Sudd. When Lake Sudd eventually filled and overflowed northward into the Nile, the modern Nile was born, connecting Lake Victoria with the Mediterranean Sea. Lake Sudd emptied and became a large, swampy area that is today called the Sudd.

The White Nile

The White Nile's source is high in the Ruwenzori Mountains of Burundi, where a mountain spring forms a stream that becomes the Kagera River. The Kagera is the largest of several rivers that flow into Lake Victoria. The one river that leaves the lake is the White Nile.

Rift Valleys

Millions of years ago, two huge cracks, or rifts, formed in Earth's **crust** along the eastern coast of Africa. The land between the rifts sank into two deep valleys, called the West African Rift Valley and the East African Rift Valley. Lake Victoria lies on the **plateau** between the two rift valleys. The White Nile runs along this plateau and then plunges into the West African Rift Valley.

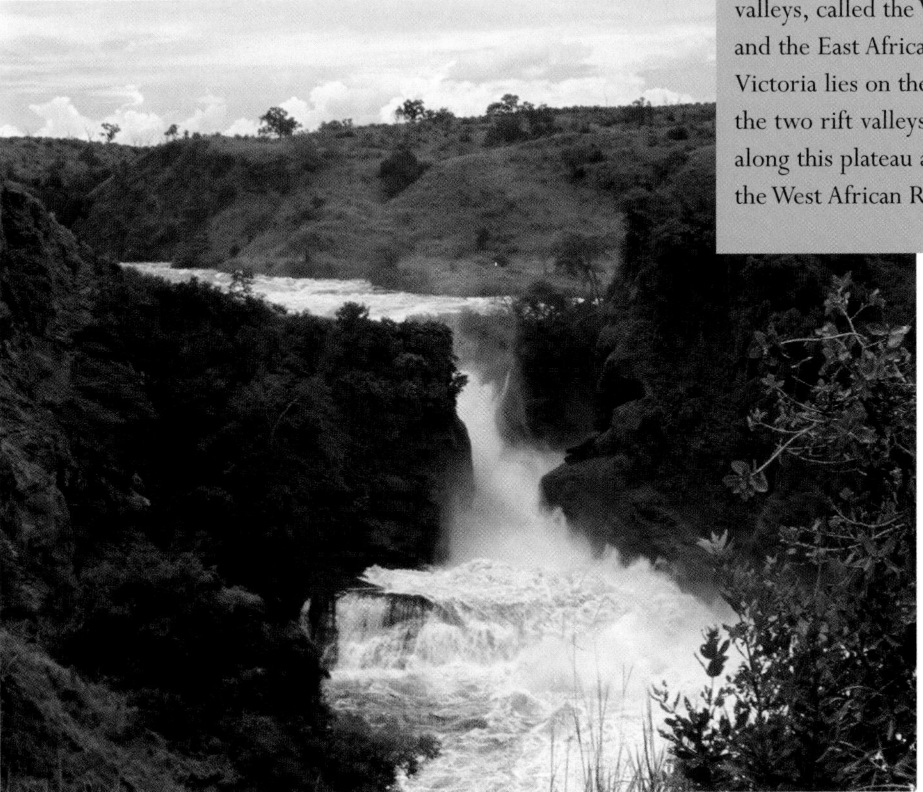

The waters of the White Nile make a thunderous descent at Kabalega Falls (Murchison Falls), located between Kyoga and Albert Lakes.

Beyond Lake Victoria, the White Nile travels through Uganda. The river passes first through shallow Lake Kyoga. Then, at Kabalega Falls (also known as Murchison Falls), it plunges 120 feet (37 meters) into the West African Rift Valley, where it flows into Lake Albert.

North of Lake Albert, the White Nile drops through a narrow **gorge** down to the plains of Sudan. In southern Sudan, the river's waters move slowly through the swamps of the Sudd — the soggy remains of the ancient Lake Sudd. Beyond the Sudd, the waters of the White Nile pick up speed on their way to meet the Blue Nile.

The Blue Nile

The source of the Blue Nile is a mountain spring in Gishe Abbay, a village 60 miles (100 km) south of Lake Tana, high in the mountains of Ethiopia. The spring is the start of the Little Abbay River, which flows into Lake Tana. The river that leaves this lake is known as the Blue Nile. As the river descends from Ethiopia's highlands, it passes through a gorge, cut by its powerful current, that is 4,000 feet (1,200 m) deep in places. It then enters Sudan. The Blue Nile supplies much of the water flowing in the Nile River.

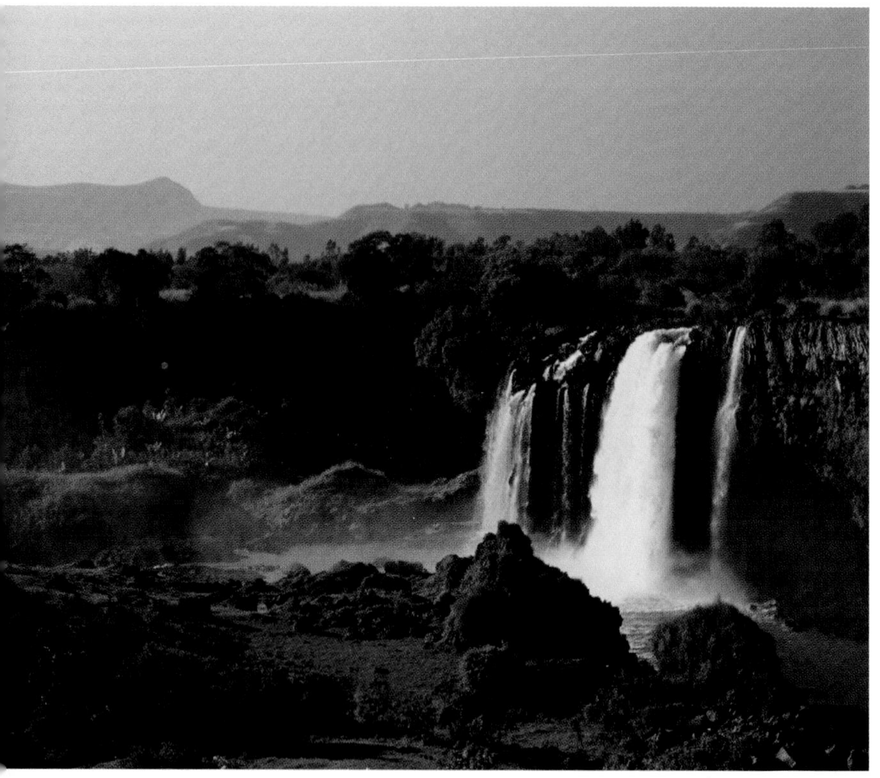

The Little Abbay River plunges down this waterfall on its way to Lake Tana.

The Nile River

Beyond Khartoum, where the Blue Nile and the White Nile form the Nile River, the Nile bends sharply to the south. The river then turns north again and passes through desert. At this point, it has many **cataracts**, or waterfalls. Near the border of Egypt and Sudan, the Nile River flows into Lake Nasser, which was formed in the 1960s when the Aswan High Dam was built across the Nile (see page 37).

After passing the Aswan High Dam, the waters of the Nile River continue northward through Egypt. At this point, the river valley is 10 to 14 miles (16 to 23 km) wide. Most of the population of Egypt is crammed into the Nile valley, where any spare space is used for growing crops. On either side of the valley, empty desert stretches as far as the eye can see. About 500 miles (800 km) north of the Aswan High Dam, the Nile flows past Cairo, the largest city on its route.

The Nile Delta

North of Cairo, the waters of the Nile River enter an area called the Nile **delta**. Millions of years ago, this delta was a deep **gulf** on the Mediterranean coast, but the gulf has long since been filled in with silt from the Nile. Layer upon layer of silt has resulted in flat, fertile land, making the Nile delta the best area in Africa for farming. The Nile enters the Mediterranean Sea through two channels in the delta: the Rosetta channel in the west and the Damietta channel in the east.

This satellite photograph shows the green, fertile plain of the Nile delta as well as the desert lands through which the Nile River flows. The large body of water on the right is the Red Sea.

White Nile and Blue Nile Facts

- White Nile: measures 2,300 miles (3,700 km) long and contributes 29% of the Nile River's water
- Blue Nile: measures 1,000 miles (1,610 km) long and contributes 57% of the Nile River's water

Riddles of the Nile

Two aspects of the Nile River puzzled the ancient Egyptians. First, the Nile never dried up, and second, the river always flooded at the end of the summer. The summer floods especially perplexed the Egyptians because the summer was their driest time of the year. They did not realize that the sources of the Nile's two branches were in different climates.

The White Nile begins in a tropical rain forest. This forest receives rain throughout the year, ensuring a regular supply of water for the river. In addition, the lakes along the White Nile's route store its water, so even if there is less rain, the water level in the river does not drop. The White Nile's steady water level explains why there was always water in the Nile River in ancient Egyptian times, even during summer.

"The Nile, when it overflows, floods not only the Delta, but also the tracts of country on both sides of the stream...in some places reaching to the extent of two days' journey from its banks..."

The ancient Greek historian Herodotus, writing in the 5th century B.C.

The Blue Nile has its source in the highlands of Ethiopia, which receive little rain in the winter. Between May and October, however, 60 inches (152 centimeters) of rain falls on the region. This large amount of rain feeds into the Blue Nile and then into the Nile River. Since the rivers cannot hold the extra water, they flood the land that is alongside them.

In June, the Blue Nile begins to flood in Ethiopia and Sudan, and by July the Nile River has begun rising in southern Egypt. It continues to rise until the middle of September. At this point in the year, the Nile in Egypt used to burst its banks. Today, however, the Aswan High Dam prevents most of this flooding.

During November and December, the water level of the Nile in Egypt begins to drop. It reaches its lowest point in March. Within a few months, the Nile begins rising again.

Controlling the Floods

In the past, the Nile flooded in Egypt at the end of the summer. The exact arrival of the floods varied, however, as did the amount of flooding. The success of crops depended on these floods. Too much water, and the crops would be washed away; too little, and the crops would die.

Ancient Egyptians kept a close watch on the Nile River so they could be prepared for either high or low water levels. They created "nilometers," which were marks cut in the riverbank to measure the river's depth. The Egyptians checked the nilometers late in the summer, when the flood waters first appeared. If the water level was higher than usual, they knew they should expect deep floods.

Since the late 1800s, dams have been built across the Nile to prevent excessive flooding. The Nile River's water level can now be controlled so that it remains the same all year round. Today, the river rarely floods in Egypt during the summer.

This farmer in the Nile delta is channeling the Nile's water into a field to ***irrigate*** *his crops.*

Chapter 2

THE NILE IN HISTORY

THE NILE IN HISTORY

An Early Civilization

One of the world's oldest civilizations was born on the banks of the Nile River in Egypt. This civilization began about 4,000 years ago, and it lasted for over 2,000 years.

Before settling along the Nile River, people in Egypt had been wanderers. Herding cattle across the region that is now the Sahara Desert, they moved from one grazing ground to another. The region was a flat grassland, or savanna, but in about 5000 B.C. its climate became hotter and it began to turn to desert. The Nile River valley eventually became the only area with plant life. As the savanna turned to sand, people began establishing permanent settlements along the Nile River.

An ancient Egyptian wall painting shows oxen being used to thresh grain. Threshing separates the grains from the stalks.

Two Kingdoms

For the next 2,000 years, villages spread along the Nile River in Egypt. The first villages were farming settlements. As the villages expanded, skills such as pottery-making and carpentry were developed. The villages gradually began to trade among themselves. This network of communities formed the basis for the kingdoms of ancient Egypt.

Two rival kingdoms gradually developed on the Nile River — Upper Egypt and Lower Egypt. Lower Egypt's territory was the Nile delta, while Upper Egypt lay to the south, along the banks of the Nile River. In about 3000 B.C., an Egyptian leader known as King Menes took control of both kingdoms. The period of a unified Egyptian civilization had now begun.

The Largest Pyramid

Name: The Great Pyramid of Pharaoh Kufu
Location: Giza, near Cairo
Date of construction: circa 2570 B.C.
Height: 450 feet (140 m)
Time to complete: 23 years
Number of stone blocks used: over 2 million
Weight of an individual block: about 2.5 tons (2.2 metric tons)

The Egyptian Empire

This civilization gradually became wealthy and powerful. The ancient Egyptian empire stretched south into present-day Ethiopia and as far north as present-day Lebanon. It was strongest during the reign of King Thutmose III (1490–1436 B.C.). After the death of Rameses III, in 1166 B.C., it began to break up. By 30 B.C., Egypt was part of the Roman Empire.

The Sphinx at Giza, near Cairo, was built about 2600 B.C. It guards the Great Pyramid, built by Pharaoh Kufu. The Sphinx has a woman's head and a lion's body.

Amazing Pyramids

Along the banks of the Nile, the ancient Egyptians built enormous stone pyramids that were elaborate tombs for their rulers. Scholars once believed the ancient Greeks invented mathematics. The ancient Egyptians, however, would have needed math and geometry to build their pyramids — long before the time of the Greeks.

Papyrus from the Nile

The ancient Egyptians made an early form of paper from **papyrus** plants, which grew in the marshes of the Nile delta. The Egyptians also developed one of the world's first written languages. They used signs and symbols, known as **hieroglyphs**, to represent sounds and ideas. Hieroglyphs were written on papyrus and also carved into the walls of pyramids and temples.

This papyrus is over 3,300 years old. It is covered with both paintings and hieroglyphs.

Early Conquerors

Today's Egyptians are descended partially from the ancient Egyptians and partially from later invaders. The first foreign invaders were the Persians, who arrived in Egypt in 525 B.C. from what is now Iran. The Persians ruled Egypt for almost 200 years. Then, in 332 B.C., they were conquered by the Greeks, led by Alexander the Great. Greek rule ended with the death of Queen Cleopatra in 30 B.C. After Cleopatra, the Romans ruled Egypt for almost 700 years.

In A.D. 642, armies from what is now Saudi Arabia conquered Egypt. These Arabs brought with them their new religion, **Islam**, and their language, Arabic. They ruled for many centuries. Arabic emerged as the language of Egypt, and the Egyptian population became mostly Muslim (of Islamic faith).

> ***"Soldiers! Forty centuries are looking down at you."***
> French emperor Napoleon Bonaparte, speaking to his troops as they stood by the pyramids waiting to attack Cairo

Later Rulers

On July 2, 1798, French emperor Napoleon Bonaparte led a French army into Egypt. Napoleon took control of northern Egypt, where he stayed for three years. During this time, he organized a detailed survey of Egypt's ancient remains. French troops were eventually forced to leave by an Ottoman army, led by General Muhammad Ali. The Ottomans were a Turkish people who built a large Muslim empire. With the support of the Egyptian people, Ali became ruler of Egypt. Ali's successors ruled badly, however, and they plunged Egypt into debt.

In 1869, the Suez Canal was completed. This important waterway linked the Mediterranean and Red Seas. The British, who helped pay for the canal, became increasingly worried that Egypt's Ottoman rulers were preventing ships from passing through the canal. In 1882, Britain took control of Egypt. This control lasted for the next seventy years.

This painting depicts Cleopatra, who ruled Egypt from 51 to 30 B.C.

Egyptian Independence

In 1922, Egypt became an independent country with its own monarch. The British, however, continued to maintain a powerful influence over the Egyptian government, and British troops remained in Egypt until 1954.

In 1952, Lieutenant-Colonel Gamal Abdel Nasser led the army in a revolt against King Farouk, the last king of Egypt. The following year, the monarchy was abolished and Egypt became a **republic**.

Sudan

The oldest ancestors of the Sudanese were the Nubians, a people who lived to the south of the ancient Egyptian kingdom. Today's Sudanese are also descended from Arab conquerors and traders who settled in the region after the Nubians.

In 1821, the Egyptians took over Sudan, but in 1881 the Sudanese rebelled against them. The Sudanese were led by Muhammad Ahmad, known as the Mahdi. The Mahdi captured Khartoum, the capital of Sudan, and he also killed the British general, Charles Gordon, who had been governing Sudan for the Egyptians. In 1898, a British army, led by General Kitchener, defeated the Mahdi. Britain and Egypt then shared joint rule of Sudan.

In 1956, Sudan became fully independent from British and Egyptian rule. Since then, Sudan has had a troubled history. The Muslim people of the north have attempted to turn Sudan into an Islamic country. The mainly Christian peoples of the south have rebelled against the northerners and have talked of separating from Sudan. Even when Sudan's peoples have not been fighting, law and order has often broken down. Amidst this instability, industries have not been functioning properly, while **droughts** in the south have led to mass starvation and death.

Ethiopia

Ethiopia grew out of an Arab kingdom called Aksum. By A.D. 100 it was wealthy and powerful, and by A.D. 330 it had become Christian. For centuries, Ethiopia remained independent while the rest of Africa was ruled by foreigners. In the 1930s, however, Italian troops invaded Ethiopia and overthrew its emperor, Haile Selassie.

Haile Selassie later returned to rule, but he became very unpopular. In 1974, he was overthrown by members of the armed forces. He died a few months after his arrest. Ethiopia was then plunged into revolution, and a group of junior army officers, led by Mengistu Haile Miriam, seized control of the country. Those who opposed the army were jailed or killed, while large numbers of the population were forcibly moved around the country to escape a famine. Every male from 18 to 70 years old had to join the army to keep Somalia from invading Ethiopia. The army was also used against the people of the Ethiopian province of Eritrea, who were seeking independence.

In 1991, Mengistu fled the country to exile in Zimbabwe. A new government, led by Meles Zenawi, began bringing democracy back to Ethiopia, and Eritrea was given its independence.

A Search for the Source

The source of the Nile River had long been a mystery, even to local Africans, but beginning in the eighteenth century, a few European explorers set out to find it. In 1770, the Scottish explorer James Bruce found the source of the Blue Nile, reaching the spring that fed the Little Abbay River. Nearly a century later, In 1858, the British explorer John Hanning Speke became the first European to see Lake Victoria. He declared the lake to be the source of the White Nile. The Scottish explorer and **missionary** Dr. David Livingstone, however, believed the Nile's source lay southwest of the lake. In 1865, Livingstone disappeared while looking for it. He was found by Henry Morton Stanley, who then found the Kagera River, which ran into the White Nile. The source of the Kagera, however, was not found until the 1930s. The Kagera River's source is now recognized as the true source of the Nile River.

"Doctor Livingstone, I presume?"

The first words of Henry Morton Stanley when he found Dr. David Livingstone, who had been missing for two years.

The journalist Henry Morton Stanley found Dr. David Livingstone. Stanley later became a great explorer in Africa.

Chapter 3

CITIES AND SETTLEMENTS

CITIES AND SETTLEMENTS

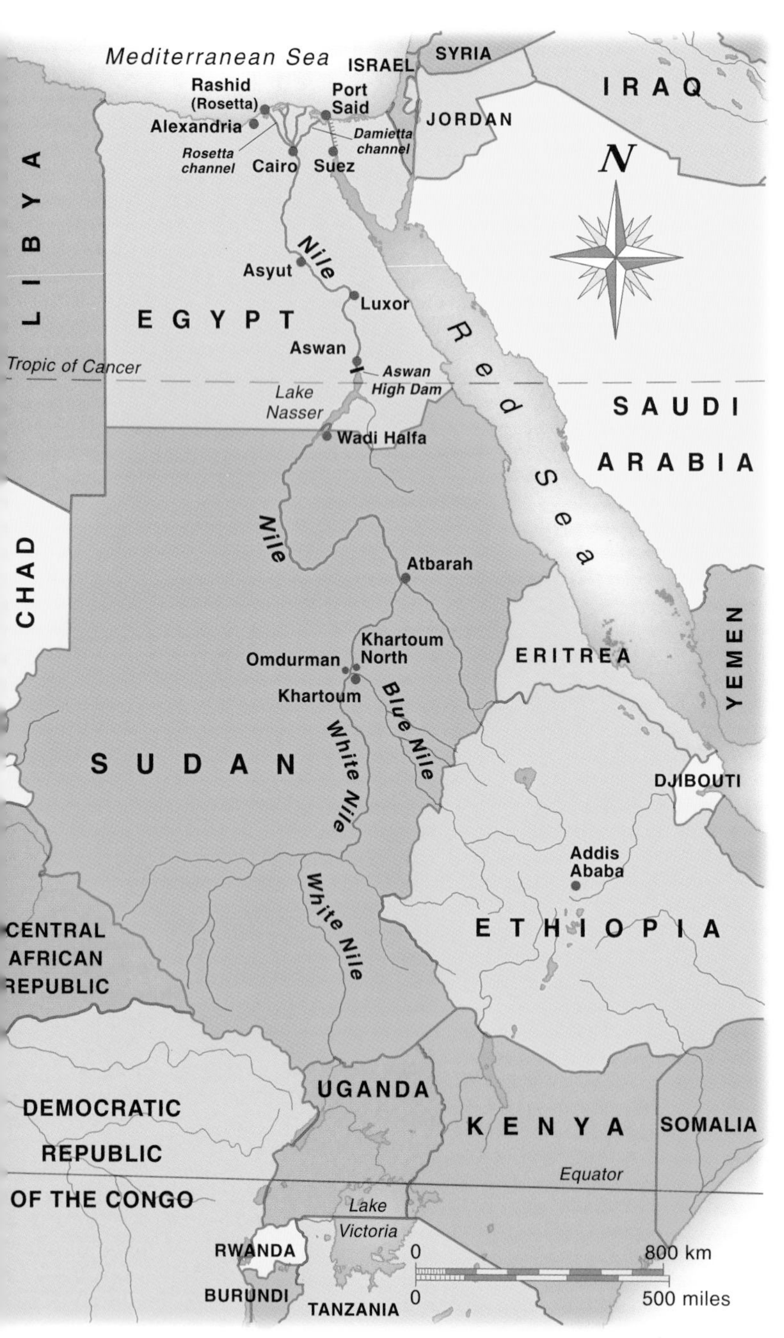

This map shows the main cities and towns along the Nile River.

Cairo (Egypt)

Cairo is located at the southern edge of the Nile delta. It is the capital of Egypt and the largest city in Africa. About 16 million people live in greater Cairo — roughly a quarter of Egypt's total population. Its Arabic name is *Al-Qahirah*, which means "victorious."

Cairo has been a city for just over 1,000 years. It has over 400 historical buildings — more than any other city in Africa or the Middle East. These buildings show the different architectural styles created by the foreign invaders who lived in the city over the centuries — the Romans, the Arabs, the Ottomans, and the British. The city's most famous sights are the pyramids built by the ancient Egyptians. The pyramids are in Giza, on the southwestern edge of the city.

The swift growth of Cairo's population has put a strain on the city's resources, such as housing and transportation. To relieve the city's population problems, the Egyptian government is building some new cities in the Nile delta.

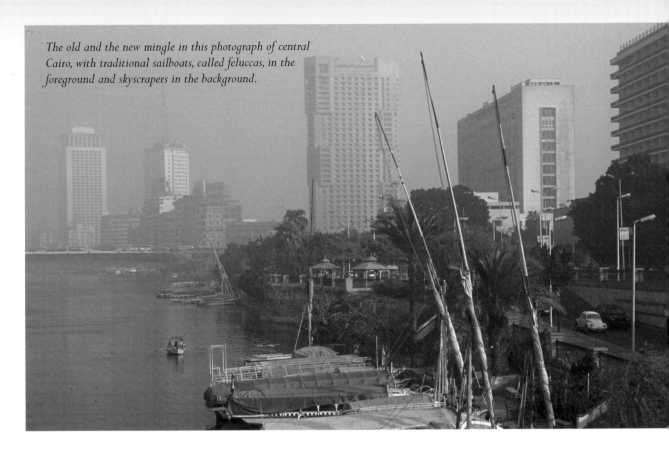

The old and the new mingle in this photograph of central Cairo, with traditional sailboats, called feluccas, in the foreground and skyscrapers in the background.

Rashid (Egypt)

Rashid is a port on the Mediterranean Sea. It is better known by its English name, Rosetta. The port became famous in 1799, when some French soldiers in Napoleon Bonaparte's army discovered the Rosetta Stone. This unimpressive piece of granite was covered with inscriptions in ancient Egyptian and Greek. The text of the two languages was identical, so experts were able to use the Greek inscriptions to translate the Egyptian hieroglyphs. The Rosetta Stone provided the key to understanding all the writings left by the ancient Egyptians.

Located on the Rosetta channel, the Nile's western branch in the delta, Rashid was once a busy harbor. In 1820, however, a canal was built that linked the channel with Alexandria. Within a few years, Alexandria had taken away most of Rashid's business.

The Rosetta Riddle

The man who unlocked the riddle of the Rosetta Stone was Jean-Francois Champollion, a child prodigy who already knew eight languages at the age of sixteen. Champollion recognized the name of the Egyptian pharaoh, Ptolemy, carved in Greek on the stone. He then realized the same text was also written in Egyptian hieroglyphs.

Alexandria (Egypt)

After Cairo, Alexandria is the second largest city on the Nile River. Located on the western edge of the Nile delta, it is Egypt's main port. At Alexandria, the cargoes of oceangoing ships are transferred to smaller vessels, which continue up the Nile River.

Alexandria has the most industries in Egypt after Cairo. The city has a population of 4.5 million. Like Cairo, it is jammed with both people and vehicles.

> ***"Alexandria, a city with 4.5 million inhabitants, has been called the world's largest village, because it does not have its own newspaper."***
> Erling Hoh, *Geographical Magazine*, April 2001

Over 2,000 years ago, Alexandria was one of the greatest cities in the world. Scholars traveled great distances to study in its library, which contained 700,000 papyrus scrolls. The scrolls were all lost, however, when the library burned down in 48 B.C.

In 2001, a new library opened in Alexandria, at a cost of $200 million. The Egyptian government hopes the new facility will attract students from all over the world.

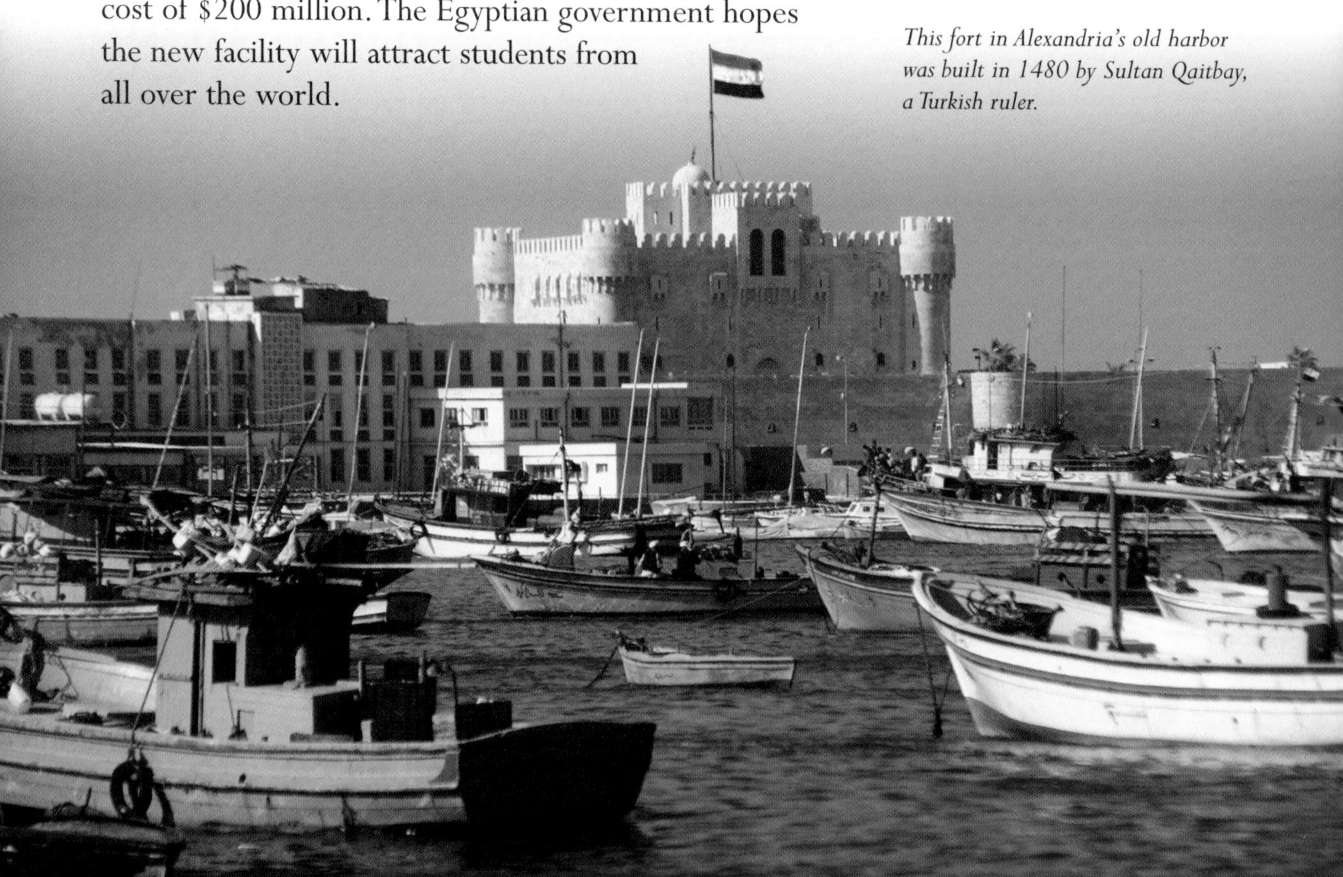

This fort in Alexandria's old harbor was built in 1480 by Sultan Qaitbay, a Turkish ruler.

Khartoum and Its Neighbors (Sudan)

Khartoum, the capital of Sudan, is located where the Blue Nile and the White Nile come together. Khartoum and its neighbors, Khartoum North and Omdurman, are separated by these two rivers. Khartoum has 600,000 people, while Omdurman has 526,000 and Khartoum North has 400,000. The three cities are linked by bridges and ferries.

Khartoum has broad streets lined with government offices and the **embassies** of foreign countries. Few of the buildings in the city are more than two stories high. On the outskirts of Khartoum, thousands of people who have fled fighting in the countryside live in **shantytowns**. Khartoum North has most of Sudan's important industries. Omdurman is full of banks and insurance companies.

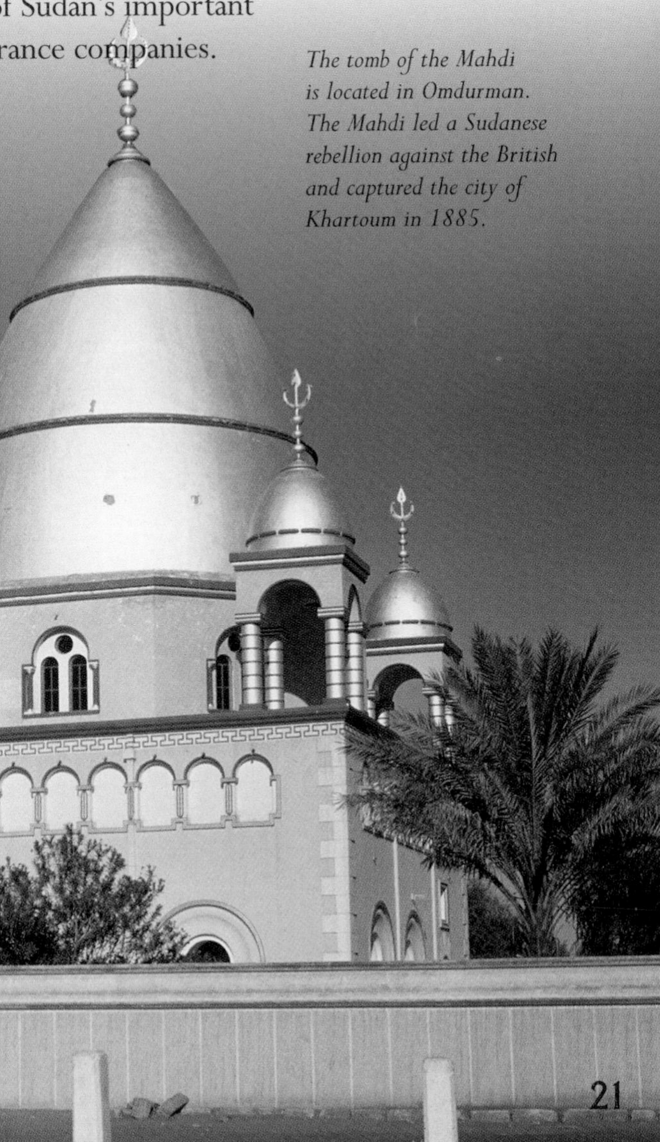

The tomb of the Mahdi is located in Omdurman. The Mahdi led a Sudanese rebellion against the British and captured the city of Khartoum in 1885.

Mud left by the Nile River has been used to build these houses in Egypt.

Village Life

The figures below indicate the percentages of the populations in Egypt, Ethiopia, and Sudan that live in villages.

- Egypt: 54%
- Ethiopia: 85%
- Sudan: 73%

Villages in Egypt

Many people along the Nile River live in villages. In Egypt, only a narrow strip of land exists between the river and the desert. With no room to expand, all the homes are tightly packed together. The houses are usually separated by alleys or narrow streets just wide enough for a cart.

The typical home in an Egyptian village has a central courtyard with high walls. It is one story tall and has a flat roof. The roof is useful for drying crops in the hot, dry climate and for storing crops away from hungry animals. In the past, Egyptian houses were built of bricks made from mud left by the Nile River's floods. The mud bricks present a problem to **archaeologists** studying ancient life in Egypt. Unlike stone houses, mud-brick houses leave no remains for archaeologists to examine.

Since the completion of the Aswan High Dam in 1970, mud for bricks has become scarce because the Nile River no longer floods. Today, villagers build their houses from bricks made in factories. The dam also provides electricity, so most village homes in Egypt have electric lights. The electricity is also used to power water pumps that bring water from the Nile to the villagers' fields.

Villages in Sudan and Ethiopia

South of the Aswan High Dam, mud continues to be left by floods from the Nile River, so houses in northern Sudan are still built from mud bricks. The bricks are dried in the sun after they have been made into the correct shape. Northern Sudan is a desert, so mud is one of the few materials available for the construction of houses.

Southern Sudan has wide, grass plains with trees. The people who live in this region have a wider choice of building materials. They usually construct round huts with a wooden frame and walls made of mud. The huts have pointed roofs made of straw or reeds. Aside from a small door, they have no openings in their walls. The huts stay cool inside.

Across the border, in Ethiopia, villages look similar to those in Sudan. People live in small round huts with walls made of earth bricks and pointed thatched roofs. Villagers spend a lot of their time outdoors, leading busy lives. The men work on the land, while the women fetch water and also find wood, the main fuel in the villages. The women spend several hours a day searching for wood, because it is becoming very scarce in Ethiopia.

Wood from forests is used to make these village homes in Sudan.

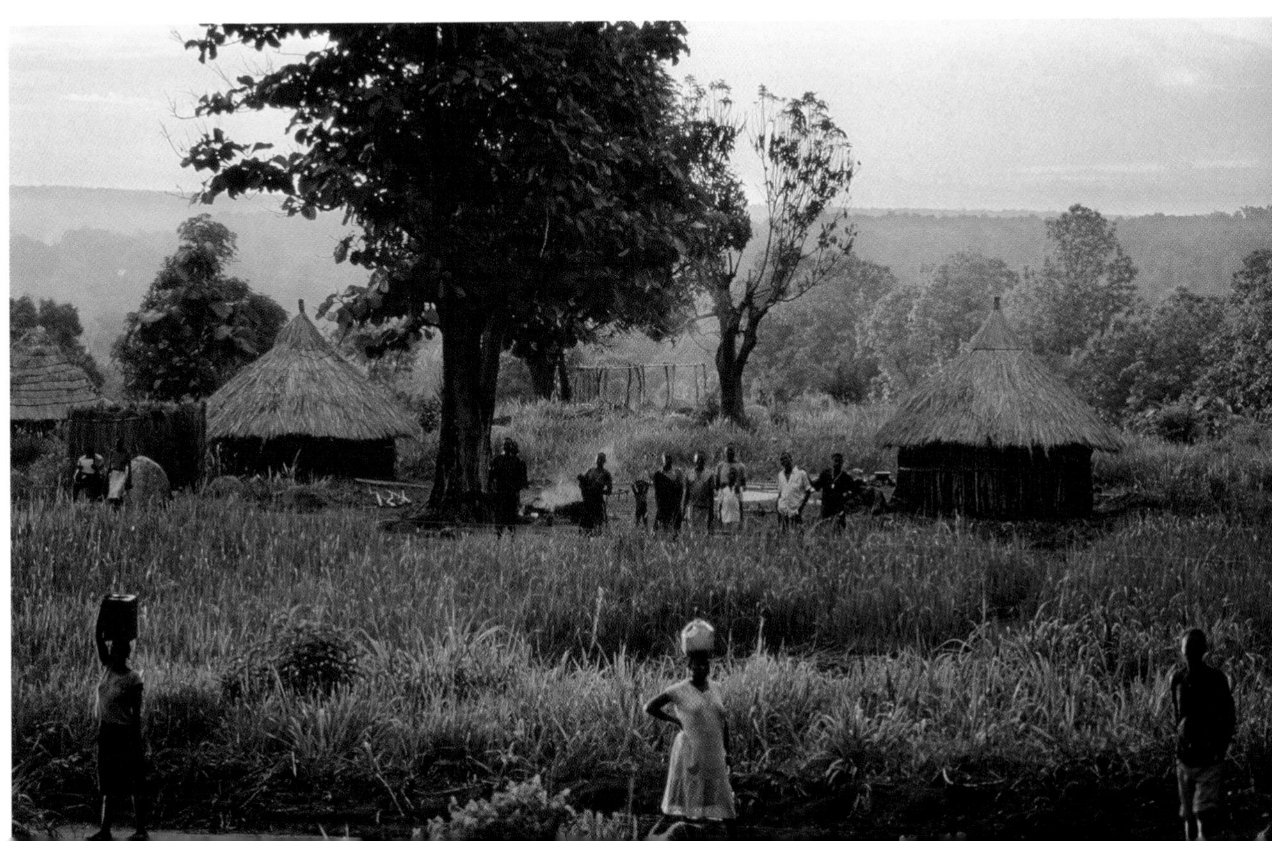

Chapter 4

FARMING, TRADE, AND INDUSTRY

Industry in Egypt

Egypt is the most industrialized country in the Nile basin. Most of its factories are in Cairo and the cities of the Nile delta. In Cairo, the largest industry is textile production. Many people work in textile factories, where they spin, dye, and weave cotton and make clothes, sheets, and towels to sell abroad.

On the outskirts of Cairo, factories produce iron and steel, as well as household goods such as stoves and refrigerators. Factories also process food crops and tobacco grown by Egyptian farmers.

At a cotton merchant's office in Cairo, cotton is bought from local farmers and sold to large companies.

The older parts of Cairo contain many workshops. The shops are usually owned by families, who make items such as wooden furniture and pots and pans. Much of the work in these shops is done by hand, utilizing skills passed down from one generation to the next.

In Alexandria, the second largest industrial city in Egypt, industries include the refining of oil into gasoline; cotton, plastic, and paper production; and food processing. About 90 percent of Egypt's imports and exports pass through the city's harbor. Cotton is the main export, while machinery, timber, and coal are the main imports.

The city of Aswan has factories producing copper, steel, chemicals, fertilizers, and cement. The city is also a busy link between Egypt and Sudan.

Industry in Sudan

Khartoum North is the main industrial city in Sudan. By the riverside, dockyards build riverboats and ferries, while nearby factories produce train engines, carriages, and wagons. The city has sawmills and cotton mills, and it also has factories for making glass and processing food. In addition, Khartoum North has many markets. Cotton, grains, fruit, and animals are all brought to these markets, where they are sold to large companies.

"My great-grandfather built this workshop, way back in the 1800s. My family has been making furniture here ever since."

Hamed Abdel Kader, carpenter in Cairo

In Egypt, most businesses are small. This craftsman is making pots and vases out of alabaster.

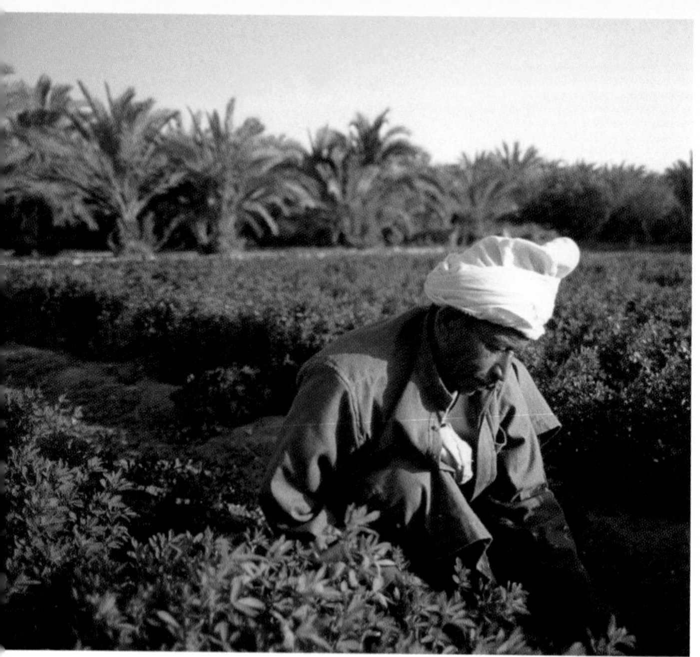

Most of the farms in Egypt are small and are run by one man with the help of his family.

Agriculture

In all the countries that the Nile River and its branches pass through, farming is an important occupation. It is especially important in Ethiopia and Sudan, where most people live off the land.

Many of the Nile River's farmers are **subsistence farmers**. They grow enough crops to feed their families but have little or nothing left over to sell in markets. These peasant farmers often do not own their fields but instead rent them from a wealthy landowner. Since they usually cannot afford agricultural machinery, they use oxen to pull wooden plows and carts.

> ***"Egypt's cotton crop is overwhelmingly the product of small farms...nearly 70 percent of cotton farmers cultivate an area of less than one acre."***
> *Human Rights Watch*, 2001

Farming in Egypt

In Egypt, peasant farmers are called *fellahin*. The *fellahin* grow a wide variety of crops — rice, corn, wheat, vegetables, and sugar cane. They also grow fruit, such as mangoes, dates, and oranges. Some farmers grow cotton for Egypt's textile industry. Egypt is one of the largest growers of high-quality cotton in the world.

Farming in Ethiopia

Ethiopia's farms are in the highlands — the lowlands are too hot and dry for agriculture. In the highlands, farmers grow coffee, corn, pulses (such as beans and lentils), and sugar cane. They also grow sorghum and teff — two kinds of grasses that produce seeds used to make cooking oil. After the grasses are dried, they are fed to farm animals. Coffee is mainly grown in Kaffa province, from which it gets its name. Most of the coffee grown in Ethiopia is sold to other countries.

Nomads

Northern Sudan, which is mostly desert, has little farming. The region is home, however, to the Kababish and Baqqara peoples — **nomads** who herd camels and goats. The Nuer, Dinka, and Shilluk peoples live in the grasslands of southern Sudan. They are also nomads, herding sheep and cattle, but some of them grow crops, such as millet and dates. In summer, the Nuer and Dinka avoid the Nile River's floods by traveling to the highlands. In winter, they return to the plains with their animals.

The Dinka people are cattle herders who live near the White Nile and the rivers flowing into it.

Fishing

Fishing is an important industry in parts of the Nile basin. It is especially important on Lake Victoria and Lake Nasser.

Fishing is big business on Lake Victoria. This lake lies between Uganda and Tanzania, with a small part in Kenya. With a coastline of 2,000 miles (3,220 km), it is Africa's largest lake and the world's second largest freshwater lake. Lake Victoria has large numbers of fish, and its fishing industry employs 30,000 people. Not all are fishermen. Many people work in lakeside factories, where they skin, gut, and freeze the daily catch of fish. Most of the frozen fish is sent by air to Europe, Japan, and the United States.

Lake Nasser

- Length: 200 miles (322 km) in Egypt, 100 miles (160 km) in Sudan
- Width: 14 miles (23 km)
- Depth: 300 feet (90 m)

These fishermen on the Nile River in Sudan are using a traditional boat and net.

Fish from the Nile River is sold at this bustling market in Cairo.

Today, Lake Victoria's fishing industry is in the hands of large companies, and local fishermen are going out of business because they cannot compete with them. The large companies have powerful boats with large nets, while local fishermen still fish the same way their fathers and grandfathers did — they paddle onto the lake in dugout canoes and catch fish with a line. The governments of Kenya and Tanzania are now considering banning fishing companies from their parts of the lake.

Lake Nasser was created in the 1960s when the Aswan High Dam was being built. The lake stretches from southern Egypt into Sudan. Covering an area roughly the size of Delaware, it is the second largest artificial lake in the world.

The dam has prevented fish from swimming up the Nile to their breeding areas, reducing the number of fish in the river south of the dam. The Egyptian government has increased fish numbers, however, by introducing new species of fish, such as the Nile perch, into Lake Nasser. Due to this effort, the lake's fishermen now catch about 98,400 tons (89,300 m tons) of fish every year.

Chapter 5

ANIMALS AND PLANTS

Rain Forest Plants

The White Nile has its source in the tropical rain forest of central Africa, a region that is warm and wet year round. Many kinds of trees — such as ebony, rubber, bamboo, and banana — grow in this rain forest. Brightly colored orchids and thick-leaved bromeliads flourish in sunny clearings, while mosses and fungi thrive in damp, shady places.

Grassland and Swamps

Once the White Nile reaches the plains of southern Sudan, the scenery changes to open savanna. This savanna is dotted with small, thorny acacia shrubs. The western half of the grassland area is the large swamp called the Sudd, which is a soggy mass of tall reeds and grasses — all that remains of the lake that existed millions of years ago.

The Sudd's grasses and reeds cause several problems. They slow the waters of the river and make it much shallower. During the hot summer, much of this slow-flowing water **evaporates**. This evaporation causes serious problems for Sudanese farmers, who need water for their crops and

The Sudd

The size of the Sudd's swamp varies greatly during the dry and wet seasons. During the wet season, it covers an area of 136,900 square miles (354,600 sq km) — about the size of Minnesota and Iowa combined. During the dry season, it shrinks to 69,400 square miles (179,700 sq km) — about the size of Missouri.

animals. In addition, large chunks of vegetation constantly break away and float down the river. These floating "islands" clog the White Nile, slowing it even more.

The Blue Nile starts its journey in the forest of Ethiopia, and it flows through a landscape that is a mixture of savanna and forest. Juniper, eucalyptus, and bamboo trees grow along the banks of the Blue Nile. In Sudan, the Blue Nile joins the White Nile just as the desert begins.

Plants and Trees in Egypt

Beyond the confluence of the White Nile and Blue Nile, the Nile River enters the desert. Except for small, scattered shrubs and papyrus plants along the edge of the river, this region has little plant life

In Egypt, farmers grow crops such as wheat, cotton, and sugar beet, as well as vegetables. Many kinds of fruit trees grow in Egypt, including orange, mandarin, banana, mango, date, and palm trees.

The banks of the Blue Nile, in the highlands of central Ethiopia, are lined with eucalyptus trees.

Birds of the Nile

Many **species** of birds can be seen along the Nile and its two branches. Some of these birds are only visitors passing through on their way to southern Africa. These **migratory** birds include swallows, ducks, and wading birds, such as the sandpiper, escaping from the cold of a northern European winter. In spring, they fly north again.

Many birds use the Sudd as a stopover point on their flight south. More than 400 bird species have been seen in the swampy Sudd, including large numbers of shoebills (also called whale-headed storks), white pelicans, and black-crowned cranes.

The forests and lakes at the start of the White Nile are home to pelicans, cormorants, storks, parrots, and tiny, brightly-colored kingfishers, as well as one of Africa's largest birds, the African fish-eagle. It dives into the lakes to grab fish with its long, sharp talons.

Of all the Nile basin countries, Ethiopia has the greatest variety of birds. More than 800 species of birds live in Ethiopia, including eagles, kestrels, falcons, buzzards, owls, and the lammergeier (bearded vulture). These birds can all be seen flying above the waters of the Blue Nile. Near the river's source, in the forests of the highlands, live yellow-fronted parrots. These colorful birds can only be found in Ethiopia.

Sacred Bird

The long-billed ibis has lived in Egypt for thousands of years. The ancient Egyptians believed the ibis was a sacred bird and linked it with Thoth, their god of knowledge. Egyptian pictures of Thoth often show him with the head of an ibis.

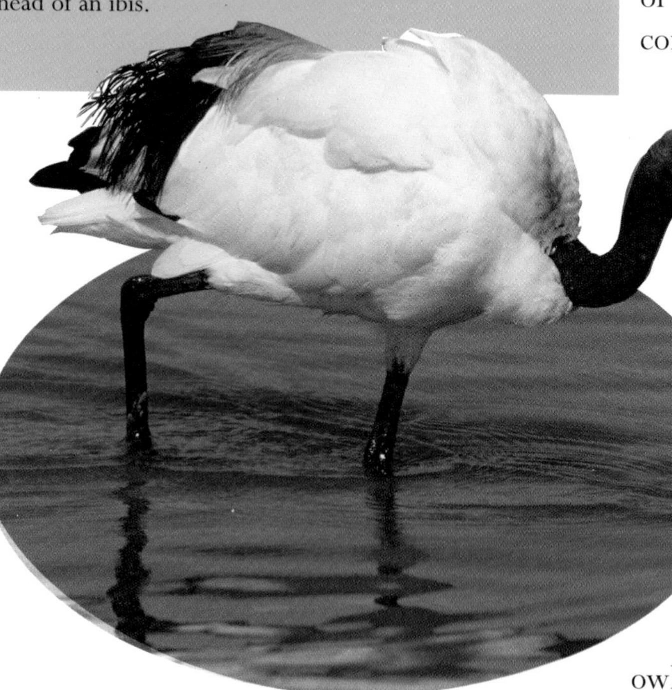

The Egyptian ibis wades through shallow water as it searches for fish.

Land Animals

The forests near the sources of the White and Blue Nile contain chimpanzees, baboons, wild pigs, and huge numbers of insects, including beetles, spiders, and soldier ants.

Many large animals can be found in the plains of southern Sudan and Ethiopia. Elephants, buffaloes, antelopes, giraffes, gazelles, and waterbucks all roam across the grasslands. For these animals, the Nile River is an important source of water. When they are drinking from the river, however, they must keep a watchful eye for crocodiles!

Camels, snakes, and scorpions live in the desert of Egypt and northern Sudan. In Egypt's Nile valley, most land creatures are domesticated animals such as cattle, buffaloes, oxen, and donkeys. Today, farmers still use animals to turn the pumps that bring water to their fields.

An elephant roams the grasslands of southern Sudan. Elephants are sociable animals and usually live in herds. They can live for up to seventy years.

River Creatures

The largest creatures in the Nile are hippopotamuses and crocodiles. Hippos were driven away from the northern Nile River by human hunters and are now found only on the White Nile. They enjoy wallowing in the shallow waters of the Sudd, where they eat the reeds and grasses.

Crocodiles are the most dangerous creatures in the Nile and its tributaries. Nile crocodiles have the most highly developed brain of any reptile, and they are very smart. A Nile crocodile swallows stones to help it digest food in its stomach. It will eat almost anything, from fish to baboons to any human foolish enough to go near it. One of its favorite meals is the soft-shelled turtle. Turtles swim slowly, so they are easy to catch.

Good or Evil?

The ancient Egyptians considered the male hippo to be evil, but they worshiped the female hippo as the goddess of birth.

The White Nile's hippos spend their days wallowing in the water. At night, they climb out of the water to graze on bushes and plants. These hippos are now an endangered species.

Few creatures survive meeting a Nile crocodile. Its jaws can crush just about anything.

NILE CROCODILE

Latin name: *Crocodylus niloticus*
Age of species: over 200 million years
Maximum length: 20 feet (6 m)
Maximum weight: 2,000 pounds (900 kg)
Maximum age in the wild: 45 years

Fish

Over 110 species of fish live in the Nile River. One of the most common is the Nile perch. A large fish, it can weigh more than 175 pounds (80 kilograms). The Nile perch is very aggressive and often attacks other fish. It also breeds very quickly. Lake Victoria once had no Nile perch, but in the 1970s some were released in the lake to increase its numbers of fish. Since then, the Nile perch have eaten almost all other species of fish in the lake, including the tilapia, which was once the lake's main fish. The tilapia is similar to the Nile perch but not as big or as aggressive.

The lungfish is the most unusual fish in the Nile River basin. It looks like an eel and lives in the marshes of the Sudd. When it has no water, it can breathe air. If the marshes dry out completely, the lungfish digs itself into the mud, where it can hibernate (go into a deep sleep) without water for up to four years.

Several kinds of catfish live in the Nile. The raad, or electric catfish, can produce an electric shock of 400 volts. Another catfish is known as the "upside-down catfish" because it spends most of its time swimming upside-down.

Chapter 6

ENVIRONMENTAL ISSUES

Controlling the Nile

For thousands of years, the Nile flooded every summer. These summer floods were welcomed by the people who lived along the riverbanks, because the floods brought water for irrigation and also provided rich soil in which crops could be grown. The floods, however, were unpredictable. In some years, heavy flooding drowned the crops, while in other years too little water caused crops to fail and often resulted in **famine**.

Since ancient times, people tried to control the Nile River so it would bring the same amount of water throughout the year. A regular water supply would allow farmers to grow crops year round and would prevent both heavy floods and crop failure.

One way to control a river is to build a dam across it. Scholars are not sure when the first dam across the Nile was built, but records show that the ancient Egyptian king Amenemhet built a dam across the river 4,000 years ago. In the 1800s, several dams were built across the Nile just south of Cairo. These dams helped prevent the Nile from flooding by diverting water into irrigation canals.

Aswan High Dam

In 1902, the Aswan Dam was completed. The first dam on the Nile to store water, it held back floodwater in an artificial lake. Water from the lake was released during the dry winter months. The dam was not high enough to keep back all the floodwater, however, so a new dam was built several miles south of the Aswan Dam. Called the Aswan High Dam, it was completed in

The Aswan High Dam was too expensive for Egypt to build on its own. The former Soviet Union provided both money and technical help for the huge project.

1970. With this dam, humans have gained almost complete control of the Nile River in Egypt.

Other Dams

Outside of Egypt, other dams have been built to hold back summer floodwater. The Owen Falls Dam in Uganda and the Jabal Awliya Dam in Sudan are dams on the White Nile, while the Sennar Dam and Roseires Dam, both in Sudan, help control the fast-flowing Blue Nile. A dam has also been built on one of the main tributaries of the Nile River — the Atbarah River. None of these dams, however, has had as much effect as the Aswan High Dam.

Aswan High Dam

Begun: 1959
Completed: 1970
Cost: $1 billion
Height: 364 feet (111 m)
Length: 12,562 feet (3,830 m)

Benefits of the High Dam

Thanks to the Aswan High Dam, the Nile River has a steady supply of water throughout the year. Water from Lake Nasser, which was formed when the dam was built, fills the Nile whenever the river's water level begins to drop. With this supply of water, farmers can grow two or three crops a year.

The dam has also created new farmland. Water from Lake Nasser is used to irrigate 1,200,000 acres (485,600 hectares) of land close to the lake. Crops can be planted on land that was once unsuitable for farming, providing food for Egypt's rapidly growing population. At the moment, only 3 percent of Egypt's land can be used for farming.

The dam has also brought additional electricity to Egypt. Water released through the dam turns huge **turbines** to create electricity. Before the dam was built, Egypt had electricity shortages, but now it has more than enough. The dam provides Egypt with 23 percent of its electricity.

Felucca owners now earn a lot of money from taking tourists on trips on the Nile.

Fishing and Shipping

Lake Nasser now plays an important role in Egypt's fishing industry, providing many people with jobs. A large amount of fish from Lake Nassar is sold in local markets, so the lake also allows Egyptians to have a healthier diet.

The Aswan High Dam has made it easier for boats to travel along the northern stretch of the Nile. Before the dam was built, the river was too shallow in the dry season for all but the smallest boats. Today, however, water levels are high enough that boats can travel from Aswan to the mouth of the Nile throughout the year. In addition, Lake Nasser has "drowned" several **rapids**. These rocky stretches of river had prevented riverboats from sailing upstream south of Aswan. Today, the water is deep enough for boats to travel over the rapids.

Farmland and People

Egypt has nearly 3.5 times more farmland now than it did 300 years ago. The population of Egypt, however, is now 26 times larger that it was 300 years ago.

Disadvantages of the Dam

For thousands of years, Egyptian farmers never fertilized their land because the Nile did it for them. Silt left behind by the Nile contained all the nutrients their crops needed.

Before the construction of the Aswan High Dam, the Nile deposited 40,000,000 tons (36,296,000 m tons) of

The Great Temple from Abu Simbel is now in its new location, high above the waters of Lake Nasser.

ELECTRICITY AND FERTILIZERS

About 30 percent of the electricity created by the Aswan High Dam is used to produce the fertilizers that Egyptian farmers spread on their land. Before the dam was built, however, the farmers did not need to use any fertilizers.

silt onto its flood plain each year. Since the 1970s, however, the silt has been trapped by the Aswan High Dam. Egyptian farmers now use 1 million tons (907,400 m tons) of chemical fertilizers each year. These expensive fertilizers put a heavy financial burden on farmers, and, since they eventually drain into the Nile, they are polluting the river.

Less silt in the lower Nile River results in fewer nutrients entering the Mediterranean Sea, so fish near the delta have a much poorer diet. Since the Aswan High Dam was built, the number of sardines in the eastern Mediterranean Sea has dropped considerably. Many sardine fishermen have lost their jobs.

After the dam's construction, the Nile River did not flow as strongly as before, so seawater has been able to force its way further up the Nile delta. Salt in this water has killed nutrients that support plant growth. Soil in the delta is easily washed away without plant roots to hold it together, so valuable farmland in the delta has been gradually disappearing.

Lake Nasser provides Egypt with a large supply of water, but it also loses a lot of water. The lake is a large body of water in a hot, dry region, and roughly 10 percent of its total water evaporates from its surface every year. This water loss is a huge waste in a country where water is such a precious commodity.

The high cost of the dam involved more than just its construction. Both people and historical buildings had to be moved to make way for Lake Nasser. About 90,000 Egyptian and Sudanese farmers were given land and homes in other places, while ancient Egyptian temples at Abu Simbel had to be carefully taken apart and then reassembled on higher ground.

Chapter 7

LEISURE AND RECREATION

LEISURE AND RECREATION

The First Tourists

Foreigners have been visiting Egypt for thousands of years, attracted by the wonders of its ancient civilization. The ancient Greeks and Romans were fascinated by everything connected with ancient Egypt, and a trip to the pyramids became part of a wealthy student's education.

After the Romans conquered Egypt, they built roads and created a police force, making travel in Egypt much easier and safer for tourists. During the time of the Roman Empire, tour guides and accommodations for visitors first appeared. Businesses offering pack animals and boats also sprang up along the Nile. Egypt's tourist industry had begun.

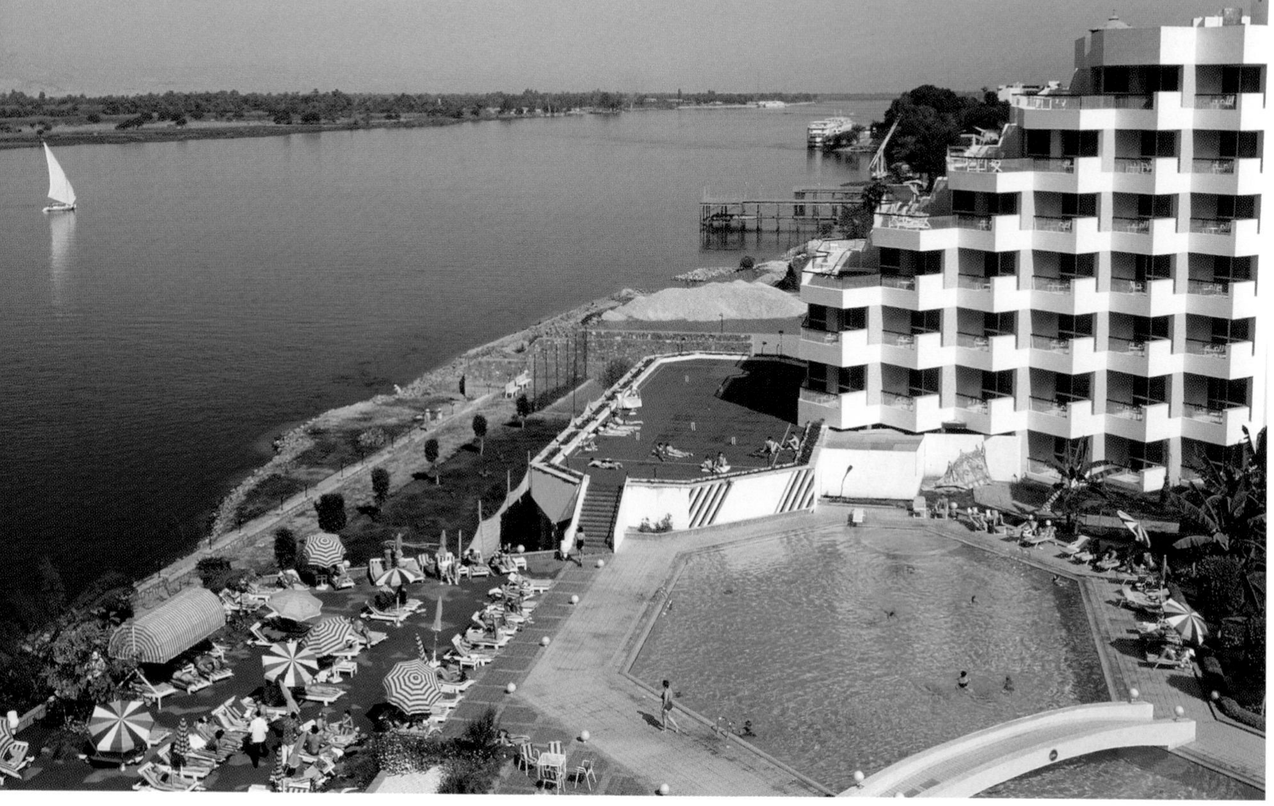

In Luxor, several luxury hotels have been built for tourists, who come from abroad and from Egypt.

Tourism Today

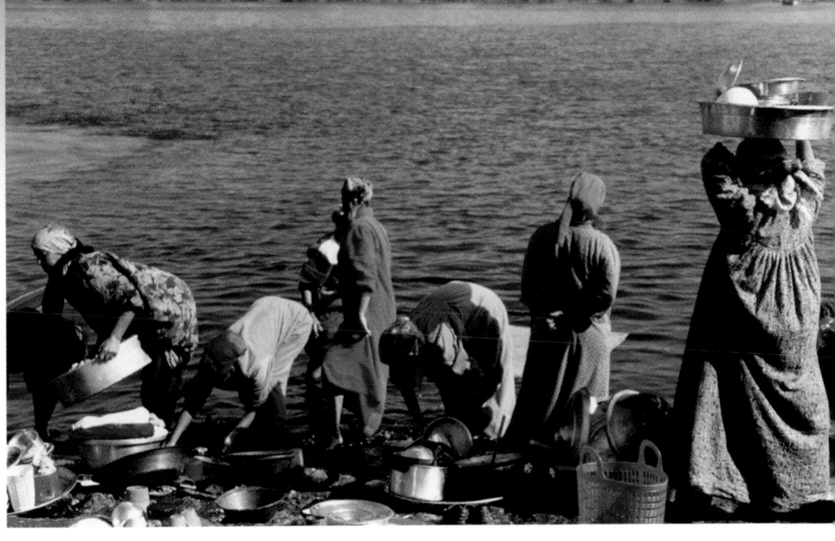

Today, tourism is an important industry in Egypt. About two million tourists travel to Egypt every year. Most tourists visit the pyramids outside Cairo, and many go on cruises along the Nile. Luxury riverboats, which resemble small, floating hotels, shuttle between Luxor and Aswan. Boats also take people across Lake Nasser to see the ruins of the temples of Abu Simbel.

Millions of Egyptians have no running water in their homes. They do all of their washing in the Nile River.

Life on the River

Foreign tourists are not the only ones who enjoy the Nile River. Wealthy Egyptians take river cruises and stay in hotels at Luxor and Aswan. Most Egyptians cannot afford such leisure activities, but they may take strolls along the riverbank with friends and family — at dusk, when the heat of the day is gone and it is pleasantly cool.

Most village homes along the Nile River do not have water piped in, so villagers (usually women) wash their clothes and pots and pans by the side of the river. To help pass the time, they chat, catching up on local affairs. Farmers wash their animals in the Nile. Truck and bus drivers also visit the river when their vehicles get dirty.

Deadly Snails

For children along the Nile, swimming in the river may be fun, but it can also be dangerous. A species of snail in the river carries bilharzia, a disease that can be fatal if not treated with drugs. About 60 percent of the children living on the shores of Lake Victoria have bilharzia, but preventing children from playing in the water is difficult. Thanks to a government awareness program, most parents now know they must take their children to a doctor as soon as they become sick.

Children who live along the Nile often use the river for recreation. Most of these children come from poor families and do not have many toys. They use the Nile for swimming and for all kinds of games.

Chapter 8

THE FUTURE

Water Wars

About five million people arrive in Cairo every day to work, making this populous city even more crowded.

Egypt, Ethiopia, and Sudan have a combined population of 150 million. By 2050, this number will have more than doubled, to 340 million. The amount of water in the Nile, however, will remain the same, and many people fear that conflicts will erupt between the countries over the sharing of the Nile River's water. To prevent such conflicts, representatives from the countries have been meeting regularly since 1993, holding conferences and creating agreements. Finding solutions, however, has not been easy.

Mistrust already exists, unfortunately, between Egypt and Sudan. Each country believes the other is taking more than its fair share of Nile water. The Egyptians claim the Sudanese have enough dams for their water needs, but the Sudanese disagree and discuss building more. The Sudanese also argue that the Egyptians take more water from Lake Nasser than they should. One-third of Lake Nasser lies in Sudan. According to an agreement between the countries, Egypt can take three times as much water from the lake as Sudan. The Sudanese, however, claim the Egyptians are using more than this amount.

Watering the Desert

In an attempt to create more usable land, the government of Egypt is now trying to turn desert into cities and farms. The government has begun work on a major project, called the Southern Egypt Development Project, that will ultimately cost about $90 billion. Upon completion, the project is expected to turn about 990,000 acres (400,600 ha) of the southern desert into farmland. The project will also provide homes for three million people. As part of this project, a 40-mile (65-km) canal is being built to take water from Lake Nasser to the southern desert.

Turning desert into farmland requires huge amounts of water. The Sudanese think the project will cause Egypt to take more water from Lake Nasser, but the Egyptians deny this assertion. They claim they are going to waste less water, so no more will be needed from the lake. The Sudanese do not believe the Egyptians and insist they will take more water from Lake Nasser if the Egyptians do the same.

People once worried about too much water in the Nile, but today they worry about too little. The countries that rely on the Nile River will need to agree on sharing its water to avoid conflict.

> ***"The Ethiopian Minister of Water Resources told delegates that unless the waters of the Nile were shared in a fair way, poverty and mistrust would continue among the countries which relied on its water."***
>
> BBC News report on a conference on the Nile basin, June 2001

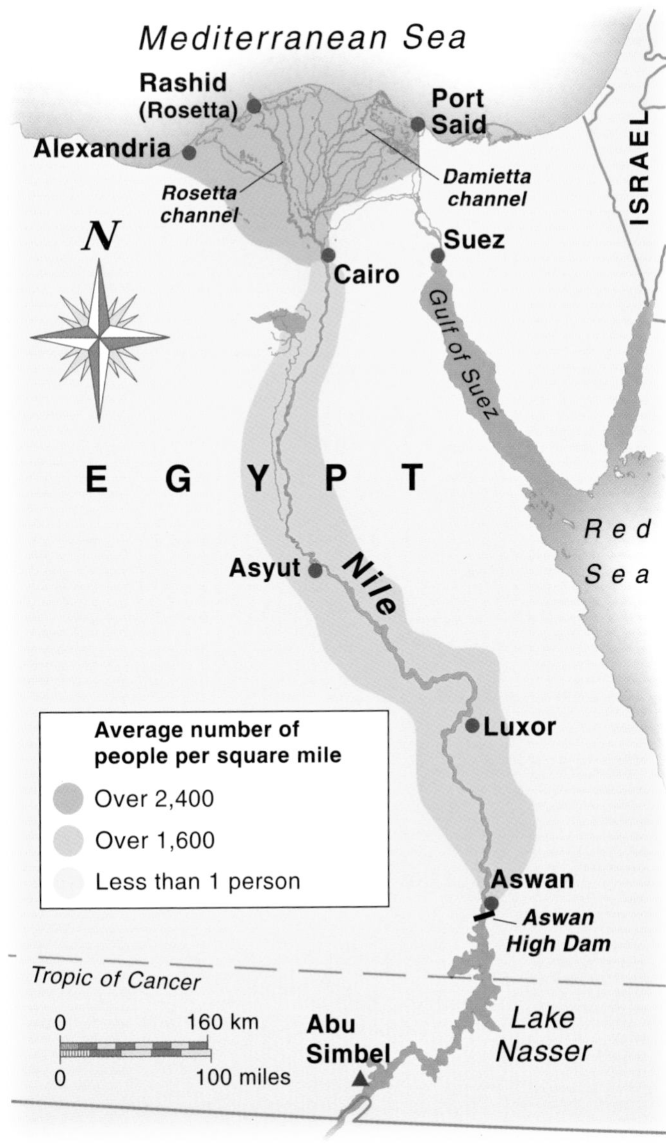

Millions of people in Egypt rely on water from the Nile. This map shows population levels in Egypt's Nile valley.

GLOSSARY

GLOSSARY

archaeologists: scientists who study human history by examining the physical remains of past human activity.

basin: the area that is drained by a river and its tributaries.

cataracts: large waterfalls or steep rapids.

crust: the outer layer of Earth.

delta: a flat, triangular area of land where a river empties into a large body of water, such as an ocean, through several channels.

droughts: long periods without rain.

embassies: buildings where representatives of a foreign country live and work.

evaporate: change from a liquid into a gas.

famine: an extreme shortage of food among a large segment of a population.

gorge: a valley with extremely steep sides.

gulf: an area of a sea or an ocean that is partly enclosed by land.

hieroglyphs: the pictures and symbols of the written language used by ancient Egyptians.

irrigate: send water to fields through channels.

Islam: a religion based on the teachings of the prophet Muhammad.

migratory: moving from one region or climate to another.

missionary: a person sent to spread a religion, often in a foreign location.

mouth: the place where a river empties into a large body of water, such as an ocean.

nomads: people who wander from one place to another.

papyrus: a tall water plant found in the Nile valley, which the ancient Egyptians used to make a kind of paper.

plateau: an area of flat land that rises above the surrounding land.

rapids: a stretch of river, filled with large rocks, where the water is extremely rough.

republic: a country that has a government consisting of elected representatives and a leader who is not a king or queen.

shantytowns: poor areas of towns or cities, usually consisting of crude shacks.

silt: small particles of dirt and rock found in river water.

source: the point of origin for the waters of a river or stream.

species: a kind of animal or plant.

subsistence farmers: people who grow enough crops to survive but rarely have any extra crops to sell for a profit.

tributaries: small streams or rivers that feed into larger rivers.

turbines: wheels that spin when their vanes, or blades, are pushed by rushing water.

FURTHER INFORMATION

TIME LINE

B.C.	
5000	People settle by the Nile River and begin farming.
3000	King Menes unites the kingdoms of Upper Egypt and Lower Egypt.
2570	Great Pyramid of Giza is built.
525	Persians conquer Egypt.
457	Herodotus, a Greek historian, travels up the Nile to modern-day Aswan.
332	Alexander the Great begins Greek rule in Egypt.
30	Romans begin ruling Egypt.
A.D.	
100	Ethiopian kingdom of Aksum reaches the high point of its power.
642	Arab armies conquer Egypt.
969	Cairo is built as Egypt's new capital.
1770	James Bruce finds the source of the Blue Nile.
1798	Napoleon Bonaparte and his army arrive in Egypt.
1882	The British take control of Egypt.
1899	Egypt and Britain begin joint rule of Sudan.
1922	Egypt becomes an independent country.
1952	Abdel Nasser leads a revolt against Egypt's last king.
1954	British troops leave Egypt.
1956	Sudan becomes independent of British and Egyptian rule.
1970	Aswan High Dam completed in Egypt.

BOOKS

Barghusen, Joan D. *Daily Life in Ancient and Modern Cairo* (Runestone Press, 2001)

Berg, Elizabeth. *Ethiopia* (Gareth Stevens, 2000)

Johnson, Darv. *The Longest River* (Kidhaven, 2002)

Meister, Cari. *Nile River* (Checkerboard Library, 2002)

Moscovitch, Arlene. *Egypt: The Land* (Crabtree, 2000)

Pollard, Michael. *The Nile* (Benchmark Books, 2000)

Roddis, Ingrid and Miles Roddis. *Sudan* (Chelsea House, 2000)

WEB SITES

Ancient Egypt
www.ancientegypt.co.uk/
A site with many fascinating facts about the ancient Egyptians.

Ethiopian Tourism
www.tourethio.com/
Information on the land, people, and history of Ethiopia.

Nile Basin Initiative
www.nilebasin.org
Facts about the Nile River basin, with many photographs.

Nile Kids Magazine
www.nilekids.net
A site for Sudanese children around the world, with facts about Sudanese traditions.

The Nile River
www.mbarron.net/Nile/
One person's site about the Nile River.

Wild Egypt: Nile
www.touregypt.net/wildegypt/nile1.htm
A well-illustrated site about wildlife along the Nile River.

INDEX

INDEX

Numbers in **boldface** type refer to illustrations and maps.